THE COLLECTOR'S GUIDE

TEDDY BEARS

CHARTWELL
BOOKS, INC.

PETER FORD

A QUINTET BOOK

ISBN: 0–7858–0542–7

This book was designed and produced by
Quintet Publishing Limited

Creative Director: Peter Bridgewater
Art Director: Ian Hunt
Designer: Stuart Walden
Project Editor: Sally Harper
Editor: Elizabeth Nicholson
Photographer: Nick Nicholson
Jacket Design: Nik Morley

Typeset in Great Britain by
Central Southern Typesetters, Eastbourne

Produced in Australia by Griffin Colour

Published by Chartwell Books
A Division of Book Sales, Inc.
P.O. Box 7100
Edison, New Jersey 08818-7100

Contents

ABOVE: *Two Bully bears, one in a sailor hat. Bully bears were created by Peter Bull and produced by the House of Nisbet.*

WHY BEARS?

AT THE TIME when the world was waiting for the teddy bear, human beings seemed at last to have come up with an idea of the bear which re-created that wild and surly creature of unpredictable reflexes into an image of total benevolence. The fascination with bears that man had felt since the bear cults of prehistory had reached its apotheosis in a child's toy. It must, moreover, have been a toy of special significance, to explain its success and the way it so swiftly established itself in the imaginations of children and their parents.

There is nothing over-simple or too obvious about the teddy bear. One of the original justifications behind its promotion held that it was a sort of 'manly' alternative doll that no little boy need be ashamed of taking to his heart. Playing with dolls would, of course, have been regarded as an unseemly occupation for boys in those days. Surveys have shown, however, that the teddy holds a secure position as the favourite toy for girls between the ages of five and ten.

Psychoanalytic theory would indeed have it that bears represent father figures. A medical director of the Institute of Social Psychiatry in London, Dr Joseph Bierer, has been quoted as saying as much before adding, 'To children they represent goodness, benevolence, kindliness. Parents who replace this cosy, unharmful toy are a menace.' Certainly bears have to take the rough with the smooth and are at times as likely to be punched and kicked as enrolled as confidantes, fellow conspirators or sources of comfort. Hence their need to display that they possess forgiving natures, while the nursery-school bully is quick to realize that one sure way of causing pain to another child is to attack it through its teddy bear.

Love and affection, warmth and softness, assurance – the giving and apparent receiving of these qualities seem to be important elements in the value of the teddy bear as a play-cum-learning toy at a certain stage of personality development. Somehow no other toy manages to do the same job in quite so evocative a way. A teddy may therefore be seen, in one sense, as

a very superior kind of security blanket, and in that sense the time comes when it is outgrown, discarded and left behind. Yet somehow our teddy bears are never wholly forgotten, and there are adults, who could never be said to be immature or especially eccentric individuals, who retain their bears through all their days and allow them to occupy a special niche in their home and family life.

Nowadays these long-standing relationships are no longer admitted to in the rather secretive or shamefaced way that was once thought appropriate. Such bears have become mascots and needed symbols of security. The teddy fancier no longer needs to fear social disapproval. Too many distinguished people are known to have shared their enthusiasm over the years, while the high prices commanded in the sale rooms make the hobby a perfectly respectable one in the eyes of the world.

RIGHT: *An appealing unmarked Teddy bear in sailor's uniform, made around 1911.*

FACING PAGE: *A well-dressed bear, the property of Barbara and Beneta Brown.*

There have been signs in the past of an anxiety that the residual native fierceness of bears could at some point reassert itself. Steiff continued to provide somewhat redundant leather muzzles to some of their bears before the First World War, but it seems doubtful whether these accessories were ever too popular as bears who still possess their muzzles are now considerable rarities. Even the words to 'The Teddy Bears' Picnic' with which we are familiar – penned by Mr Jimmy Kennedy in 1930 – contain the cautionary notion that if our bears were to get off somewhere together on their own, then feral tendencies might well surface.

In fact it is only occasionally that models of toy bears reach back to create a representation of the bear's true animal nature. Strictly speaking, bears of this sort, however well they are designed and crafted, cannot be regarded as true teddies. The classic figure of *Bruno edwardus* stands out stalwartly and independently. In trying to define the classic bear we shall find ourselves moving steadily further from naturalism for the teddy bear is nothing if he is not a stylized creation.

DEFINING THE CLASSIC BEAR

There are, to begin with, the bears that may be regarded as proto-teddies, though examples of these are few and far between. Among them is a little brown bear, with large ears set low down at the side of his head, that was auctioned at Sotheby's in London in 1984. He was known to date back to before 1903 as his provenance was vouched for by an old lady, by then in her 90s, who had been given him when she was a baby. There were also the so-called 'Peter' bears, manufactured by the firm of Gebrüden Süssenguth at Coburg in Germany. It is often stated for a fact that these particular bears, with their rocking eye and tongue mechanisms and realistically painted teeth, were only manufactured between the years 1925 and 1928, after which they were dropped from production.

This provides an example of how all 'facts' must be treated with caution in questions of teddy bear lore. Pam Hebbs has shown, with the backing of documentary evidence, that a range of these bears was featured in the original

Süssenguth catalogue of 1894. What is beyond all doubt is that they lived up to their maker's claim to be 'most natur-like' *(sic)* with their fur finish, rolling eyes and tongues and displayed teeth, and that as a result they made somewhat alarming nursery companions. A rare and valuable example of a 'Peter' bear was once given to Peter Bull to add to his hug, but it proved to be most unhuggable and not an easy bear to share a home with, and in the end he disposed of it.

What is claimed to be the original Mitchtom 'teddy bear', presented by the Roosevelt family, sits in a glass case in the Smithsonian Institute in Washington, but it is a claim that has come under much critical fire from experts. Whatever the truth in this matter, it is the Steiff bears that set the general standard for the earliest teddy bears, and the resemblance is close between them and all those other bears which are their contemporaries. The Steiff bears were highly distinctive but also immensely influential. It may even be true that certain small bears in particular have in the past been auctioned as Steiffs when they were the products of other firms whose names are by this stage unidentifiable or even forgotten. The great majority of early bears were made either in Germany or the United States, and the Steiff bears were among the top sellers. The way a Steiff bear looks is therefore the first thing with which any collector ought to become familiar. It needs to be empha-

sized that it is impossible to make too close a study of bears and their different characteristics as these have been introduced by their makers at various periods.

The profile of the early Steiff bear runs as follows. He gazes at us with black boot-button eyes along a sharpish muzzle, trimmed of its plush, that ends in a well-stitched wool nose above an inverted 'V' for a mouth. He has a distinctly humped back to testify to his origins in the wild. His arms are long, and as he stands there, between perhaps 18 and 30 inches (45 and 75 cm) high, they hang down almost to where his knees would be if he had any. His front paws and feet are large, his legs taper towards his feet from broadly placed thighs, his feet are set at right angles to his legs, and his claws or toes may well be represented by black wool stitches. All his limbs are jointed and movable, attached sideways on at the shoulders and hips. He can sit with his legs stretched out or he can raise his paws above his head if he wishes, or else he can stretch out his arms in an appealing gesture. In so doing he will display the felt or velvet pads on his paws and feet.

His head pivots in a similar way to his limbs and he has the great advantage of being able to turn it through 360 degrees so he can look backwards behind him. The rather loose type of jointing that was originally used for his movable parts was, incidentally, quite soon to

FACING PAGE: *A pair of early Steiff bears to whom time has given a touching individuality.*

ABOVE LEFT AND RIGHT:
The profiles of the smaller and the larger bear respectively.

be replaced by an improved system using discs or stiff cardboard. His fur is, as a rule, made of mohair plush (a fabric distinguished from velvet by its longer and looser pile) in a range of natural shades from beige to brown, and his rather unyielding body is stuffed with wood shavings or sawdust. Excelsior was the proprietary name for a patented type of fine, curly wood shavings much used in early stuffed toys. Sometimes his stomach is fitted out with a 'growler' that, if it is still in working order, emits a noise when he is turned on his head, though the noise itself has in some quarters been considered a bit of a joke since it sounds more like a cow mooing than anything else.

ABOVE LEFT: *A Steiff button survives* in situ *in its owner's left ear.*

BELOW LEFT: *A pair of Steiff bears in blond plush dating from 1908.*

LEFT: *An early large Steiff bear with gangling limbs, c 1904.*

There is one other detail which needs to be mentioned. He has a metal button in his left ear. This is the famous *Knöpf im Ohr* ('button in ear'), a registered trade mark device settled on by Margarete Steiff in 1904 to reassure customers that such bears were genuine products of her workshops. The button originally held a label in place, and it might be blank or it might have the name 'STEIFF' die-stamped on it in capital letters. It is very likely to be made from a pewter alloy. Most labels and many buttons were probably detached by parents, for safety's sake, before the bears were handed over to children, but examples do occasionally emerge with labels as well as buttons intact. It is more common for the button alone to still be in position, but in the course of events many genuine Steiff bears are today buttonless. It has also been known for straying Steiff buttons to become attached to the ears of non-Steiff bears in the hope of raising values. The Steiff button does therefore have its problematic aspects for the collector.

The above portrait of a bear is a generaliza-

FACING PAGE: *Two bears owned by Barbara and Beneta Brown.*

tion, and it has to be remembered that variations on the basic specifications start to appear from the very beginning. It nevertheless represents the fundamental pattern, back to which all later developments need to be related.

We have so far referred to the bear as 'he' in line with the father-figure theory, and most owners of bears will tend to think of their unclothed charges as 'Mr' rather than 'Mrs'. It would be a bad day for bears though, if the contentious issues of sexism were to surface in the world of arctophilia. Teddy bears are on the whole remarkably androgenous figures, as dressing them in different styles of clothes will demonstrate. They are only too willing to be whatever gender their owners would like them to be and can on the whole look as convincing in a frock as in trousers. Manufacturers have, in more recent years, tried to come up with 'gentleman bear' and 'lady bear' casts of face

for ready-dressed models or families of bears.

Labels, trade marks and tokens may clearly be of the utmost importance in dating examples of bears, as may changes and developments in their physical characteristics. These questions will be gone into in more specific detail in Chapter Eight. Meanwhile we are mainly concerned with the broad outline of bears, and the phases it has passed through to produce the bear that would be recognized as typical by the greatest number of people today. The focus here, for various reasons, must be on the way the bear evolved between the First and the Second World Wars. Social circumstances have had their influence on bears, especially in times of war, when traditional trading patterns have been interrupted and manufactured materials have been in short supply, but the bear was changing slowly and surely in any case.

If the bear craze had its beginning in the

ABOVE: *Clockwork Byng bear on a swing, c 1910.*

RIGHT: *A group of pre-1930 Schuco bears of assorted colours.*

United States in 1902 and spread to Britain a while later (the term 'teddy' emerges in no trade catalogues in Britain before 1909) it was not really damped down until the outbreak of the First World War. By that time bears had literally begun to take on a new look. Boot-button eyes, stitched into place, had given way to glass eyes with pupils, anchored into the head by long spikes or wires. Various later dates than this have sometimes been authoritatively put forward for the introduction of glass eyes, but a Sears Roebuck catalogue for 1912 states that its finest quality German plush bears were at that time 'all fitted with glass eyes'.

The range of shades used to make a bear's fur had widened and in some cases become quite unusual, but the main changes did not really get going until the return of peace in the 1920s. Teddy bears then took their place in the flapper age and colourful wardrobes became quite the fashion. Providing bears with complete outfits of clothes was nothing new in itself however. That had begun to happen in the earliest days of the teddy bear craze in 1906. The overall profile also started to change after the war, the hump at last beginning to modify (though not yet to disappear entirely). The limbs began to shorten, the feet to become less prominent (by the end of the 1930s), and the torso to grow stouter in outline. Rexine began to replace felt or velvet on paw pads, while noses at times grew black and hard when they happened to be made from gutta-percha. When the hump finally went out of vogue, some elderly bears found themselves being let in for plastic surgery.

As rounded curves became far more popular for bears, the bear profile softened, as did the types of stuffing used to pad him out. Kapok by this time began to be used far more widely. The result was all the while moving towards a more cuddly bear and one that might suffer no hurt if he should, for instance, fall off the ottoman or get dragged bumping down the stairs. Intimately involved in all such developments was one particular highly influential bear:

> *Our Teddy Bear is short and fat,*
> *Which is not to be wondered at.*
> *A bear, however hard he tries,*
> *Grows tubby without exercise.*

He still had a bit of a hump, as the drawings of him by E. H. Shepard showed, and his name

ABOVE: *A group of Judith Sparrow 'Big Theodore' resin bears.*

of course was Edward Bear, alias Winnie the Pooh. A A. Milne's four classic children's books were published in the 1920s in this order: *When We Were Very Young* (1924), *Winnie the Pooh* (1926), *Now We Are Six* (1927) and *The House at Pooh Corner* (1928).

The eponymous hero of the two sets of Pooh stories therefore became for several generations a special and particular image of what a bear should be, though Shepard made him such a strong individual that he could never have been mistaken for any other bear. Winnie the Pooh is thus both unique and representative.

The original model for the stories was

ABOVE LEFT: *Close-up of Brother Ted, a jester bear of 1927.*

BELOW LEFT: *Brother Ted shows off his motley colour scheme in a full-length portrait.*

Christopher Robin Milne's own bear, which was close in appearance to the Steiff standard for bears. When he came to draw the character, however, E. H. Shepard used 'Growler', his own son's bear – a 1906 Steiff bear, it so happens – as his starting point, and developed Pooh creatively from there. The well-rounded bear that emerged from the Pooh revolution was to provide the foundation for the next generation of bears in the years following the Second World War.

Any one impression of a 'classic' bear is always essentially transitional, but if the 1920s and 1930s were the hey-day of the classic bear, then the shadow of the basic Steiff is still there behind it, to help us maintain a definitive notion.

When that indefatigable arctophile Peter Bull was invited by a toy firm, the house of Nisbet, to come up with the specifications for his idea of the perfect teddy, free from all gimmicky accretions, he went for a long muzzle and a hump and 'that woollen embroidery for the pads and the paws'. The fact that children liked 'to

pick at the embroidery and then it's hell for the poor parent to knit on again' was, in his view, all part of the fun. The result was Bully Bear, a classic teddy if ever there was one, launched commercially by a party at the British House of Commons in October 1980. Time and time again, whenever we try to pin down the classic features, we find them in the original bear that Richard Steiff designed for his Aunt Margarete.

BELOW: *A Steiff wheeled bear, meant to be ridden on, c 1918. He is steerable and provided with a ring-pull growler.*

TALL, SHORT AND MOBILE

The classic bear in his ascendancy had three other manifestations: the large bear, the miniature bear and the bear on wheels. The large bear could be large indeed, as large as, or larger than, his owner. He could be a piece of conspicuous vulgarity standing maybe four or five feet (one and a half metres) tall. Some were manu-

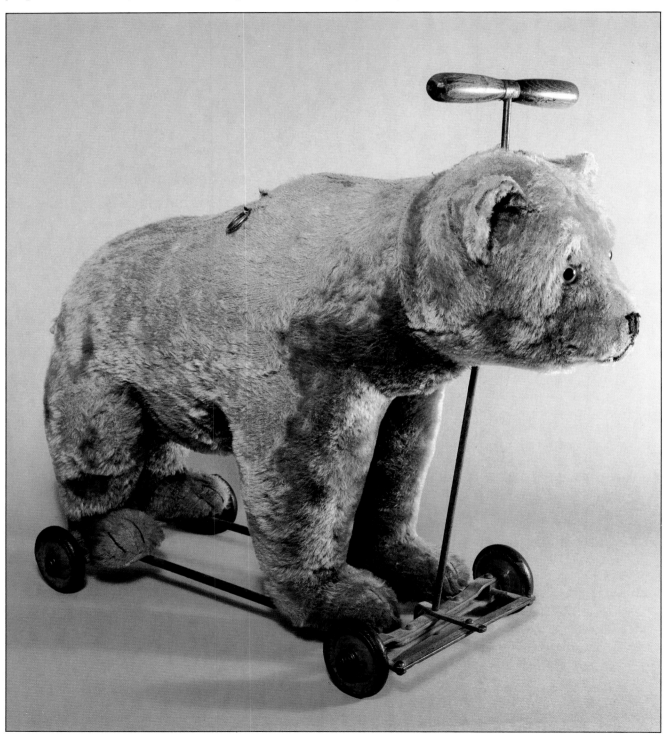

factured to be centre pieces for trade displays in the toy departments of big stores before Christmas and sold to ostentatious nurseries.

The miniature bear, by contrast, had a far more cultivated pedigree. Steiff was producing bears as small as nine inches (22 cm) high by 1905, but the true miniatures are six inches (15 cm) or less. In the 1920s the Nuremberg firm of Schreyer was producing a notably characteristic type of bear that was only 2⅜ inches (6

cm) high, built on a rigid patent metal frame but covered in soft mohair.

The bears on iron wheels were made large enough for a child to ride on their backs, and were altogether closer to the wild bear, being down on all fours. Sometimes they were covered in blanket material, but the better-quality ones had coats of mohair plush. Steiff had always produced a range of wheeled animals, so naturally there were bears among them.

ABOVE: *Paddington Bear and his Aunt Lucy make the acquaintance of a newly dressed and sinisterly smiling Sussengüth 'Peter' bear.*

ABOVE: *German automaton dancing bears on a wind-handle musical box as well as a wind-up tinplate walking bear.*

THE MOVING BEAR

THE HISTORY of the automated bear is more closely tied in, at the outset, with the development of the automaton toy than with the history of *Bruno edwardus*. There were reputedly automata in Ancient Greece, while in eighteenth-century Europe clockmakers built ingeniously devised and much-admired mechanical men. Automation in toys is something that has always followed close on the heels of wider developments in science. It can perhaps be seen as a relatively frivolous application of serious new technological principles or inventions. Clockwork toys of enamelled tin, cheaply mass-produced and as often as not made in Germany, became common nursery ornaments during the later Victorian era. Among the manic clowns, the performing dogs and cats, the trick cyclists, jugglers and acrobats, there were also bears which went through their acts and stunts. Any one of these today will be highly prized as a collectors' piece.

It becomes clear that collectors of bear material cannot always expect to have an exclusive interest in the field. At certain points they are going to find themselves in direct rivalry with collectors in other areas. A performing or dancing bear is going to represent as choice an item for the collector of tin automata as it will for the bear enthusiast. All such vintage items are attractive and charming and cannot fail to bring out acquistive instincts in the eyes of those who spot them in sale rooms and specialist shops. Therefore prices are high today, especially for well-preserved pieces in working order.

The bear was, in this context, only one animal in a whole menagerie of examples. If we are now singling out the bears it is because of the attention they have drawn to themselves through the extraordinary teddy bear phenomenon. The same comment may be said to apply to those wall-hanging, wood-crafted toys with movable limbs that jerk up and down when you pull a string attached to their backs. Sometimes the motif used for these was a bear, especially in Russia, and toys in the form of a bear have added collectability.

There was also, however, another type of mechanical toy that was specifically a bear, individually built and given a covering of authentic fur to hide his mechanism. Originally these sometimes startlingly realistic creations performed technical displays that were intended

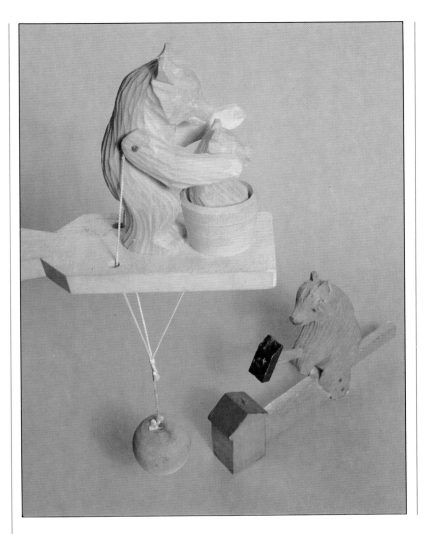

RIGHT: *Two wooden carved Russian bears. The one with the wooden ball moves its arms and washes its young in a tub; the other works by a push/pull device to bang in a nail.*

much more for the drawing room than for the nursery. Mass-produced versions soon followed, including among them bears that would walk on all fours or on their hind legs, bears that would dance, bears that would climb ladders, tumble on the floor or perform somersaults on a trapeze.

Outstanding examples of such bears were produced by the German firm of Gebrüder Bing of Nuremberg, kitchenware manufacturers who branched out into tin clockwork toys at about the turn of the century. Bing bears, fully mechanical or simply with jointed limbs, were quite close to the Steiff convention in appearance, though with smaller ears and slightly flatter noses. They also had a metal tag clipped on to their ears – rather like the identification tags farmers use on cattle today. At first the tags had the initials 'G.B.N.', which stood for Gebrüder Bing Nürnberg, though soon after the First World War this was changed to 'B.W.' for Bing Werke. Bing bears were renowned

for being splendidly and colourfully dressed, but they are rare and valuable enough as they stand and examples with their original clothes intact are few and far between indeed.

The Bing company went into liquidation early in the 1930s, but mechanical bears continued to be manufactured by the toy industry, latterly by the Japanese, in great quantities until the reign of the clockwork toy began its final decline in the 1960s. Along with so much else in the lives of succeeding generations, the key-wound clockwork mechanism became an outmoded piece of technology, ready to be replaced by friction gears and battery-powered electronics.

THE TALKING BEAR

The Sussengüth bears, already described in the previous chapter, possessed a simple automated feature in their moving eyes and tongues. The most rudimentary piece of automation of all, however, was the 'growler', the device in the

ABOVE: *A pipe-smoker and a drummer: two Japanese battery-operated tin automaton bears.*

stomach to enable a bear to make a theoretically growly noise when he was rocked from side to side or turned topsy-turvy. Sometimes squeakers were used instead, which put out a noise whenever the stomach was pressed in. A venerable bear, needless to say, will not always have a growler or squeaker in operative order.

Growlers went through various stages of improvement after the early rather unsatisfactory Steiff ones, and in the 1920s the English firm of Chad Valley was producing ranges of bears which were fitted with what was called the 'Chad Valley patent growler'. Squeakers and growlers come to seem exceedingly primitive devices in comparison with later developments. The most recent chapter in the history of the growler in fact is the techno-bear of the present day, whose insides conceal a micro-chip cassette player that equips him with a vocabulary of up to 400 words in variable order.

Such gimmicks would doubtless have been deplored by the late Peter Bull, for whom the whole business of communication with bears took place on an altogether more elevated plane of the imagination. As a general principle, of course, classic toys of all types have a wonderful simplicity that represents a challenge to a child's imaginings and is most important in the development of those capacities. The marvels of science let loose in the land of toys can all too often be an impoverishment rather than an enrichment: an adult notion of what a child ought to like rather than what a child actually needs. In this respect, Peter Bull's instincts would most certainly be correct. The irony is that, in a deep sense, a chatterbox bear may be far less effective as a communicator than a bear which sits and looks back at you with boot-button eyes. The bear, as a highly developed marketable novelty product, actually seems to be in the process of losing his human appeal. In the end that appeal surely all depends on the qualities of the classic bear, however much that bear may have lost bits of his stuffing.

ABOVE LEFT: *A fierce-looking open-mouthed clockwork walking bear with a coat of real fur.*

BELOW LEFT: *A tricycle bear and a scooter bear, both dating from the 1930s.*

In their book *Teddy Bears*, the French bear historians, Geneviève and Gérard Picot, give an account illustrating the appeal of the techno-bear in certain adult circles. They describe an occasion when prototype bears of two different sorts were handed out to delegates at a conference in the United States.

Those given to the men were dressed in a pin-striped suit, white shirt and red tie and, when activated, said in a deep voice: 'You are on the path to success, you're a born winner.' Women were given bears dressed in a white suit with a striped red blouse, and which gently murmured: 'Be what you want to be. You're perfect, absolutely perfect. Mr Bear says you're a winner.'

It seems a sad day when we hear of teddy bears being dragooned into telling the yuppie generation not the truth about itself but only what it wishes to hear. It is even sadder to learn that these craven bears achieved over half a million in sales.

NOVELTY AND LISTENING BEARS

The novelty bear began to put in an appearance early on in the days of the bear craze. In the years leading up to the First World War, Pam Hebbs tells us, bears became capable of all manner of activities: 'they growled, they cried, they nodded their heads, they ran on wheels. There were teddy bears whose eyes lit up electrically.' Peter Bull in his book *Book of Teddy Bears* quotes a firm called the Fast Black Skirt Company as advertising in this period 'Electric

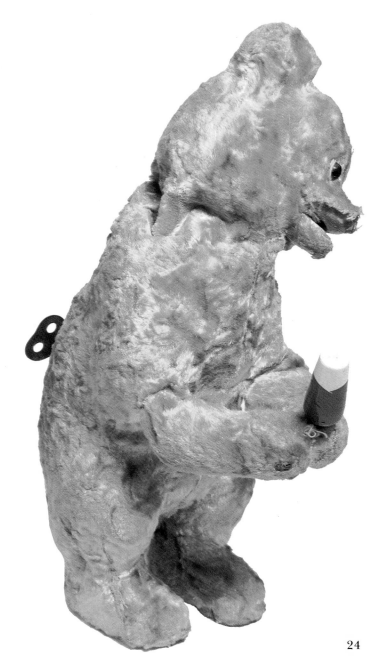

LEFT: *Two mechanical bears: one can knit, the other can read.*

Bright-Eye Teddy Bears – Shake the Right Paw, Eyes Light Up White or Red'.

The onset of the war called a temporary halt to the flow of innovation, but it was on the move again soon after peace was declared. The 'electric eye bear' itself clearly continued to represent a thoughtless hazard for small children – a case of ingenuity outstripping basic safety requirements. The Sears Roebuck catalogue for 1919 included an emphatic statement on why the company would neither stock nor sell such bears: '. . . up to the present, we have not found one that will give entire satisfaction. The batteries soon wear out and the small bulb glass eyes break easily. We recommend plain bears.'

It was also at about the close of the war that the firm Schreyer und Co. built a new factory in Nuremberg to specialize in the manufacture of mechanical toys as well as of the famous miniature bears already described in Chapter Two. Through the company's trademark,

'Schuco', their range of bears came to be known as Schuco bears, the so-called 'Yes/No' bear being a product that was specific to the company. By twisting the tails of these bears, you could make their heads nod for an affirmative or shake for a denial. Certainly this engagingly simple device opened up possibilities of games that might be played with bears, such as asking whether one's porridge was still too hot to eat, and they continued to appear in various manifestations. One of the most appropriate of the 'Yes/No' bears was the bell-hop bear, who was dressed in a smart red jacket and the round red cap of a hotel page. An alternative version was a bear whose tail merely made the head swivel so he seemed to be looking about the room (a 'No/No' bear).

Apart from these there were, among others, the usual walking or somersaulting bears and a skating bear who would have looked very fine as he used the linoleum as a skating rink. The trade-name 'Schuco' appeared on the keys used

RIGHT: *A musical-box bear with a train that goes round and round to the accompaniment of a Disneyland tune.*

BELOW: *The 'Minic' walking bear, with original box, manufactured by Triang.*

to wind the clockwork, but in the nature of things the majority of these have been lost. Schuco bears are, even so, highly recognizable for their jaunty panache and excellent quality.

Schreyer's went into eclipse in 1936 because the toys, together with their originators, fell victim to the Nazi persecution of the Jews. The firm of Schreyer was revived in the postwar years and achieved considerable sales in North America through one of the directors, who had managed to escape from the terror in Europe, and had set up a subsidiary import company in the United States. Schuco bears from all periods are today highly collectable items.

When Schreyer's eventually went into liquidation in the early 1970s, it was because they could no longer compete with the boom in toy-making that originated in the Far East, from Japan and Taiwan in particular. Since the 1950s, Japanese toymakers had been vigorously exporting to the world all sorts of clockwork bear automata, including such devices as shoe-shine bears and bears that sit writing at desks. Good examples of these, too, have now come to be firmly ensconced under the heading 'collectable'.

It needs to be said that Steiff have also made mechanical and tumbling bears at various times, as well as bears with voice boxes and musical bears that may be regarded as an extension of the voice-box principle. Some bears may essentially be music boxes dressed up to look like teddies. In examples of earlier tin-plate toys, the bear may be simply a revolving ornament on top of a musical box. Other bears are little

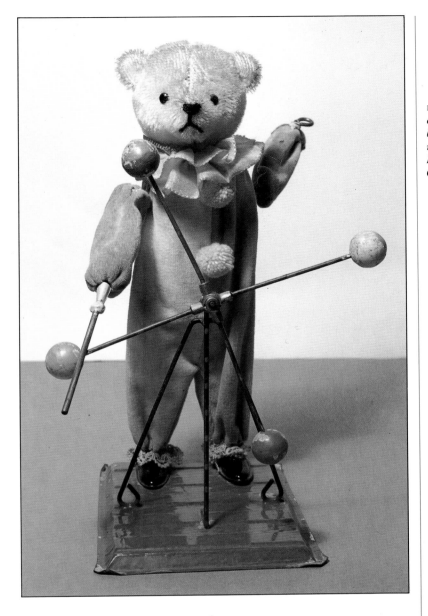

more than a particularly fancy kind of alarm clock. Yet other bears have hearts that beat inside their chests, while the introduction of the cassette player into doll making has meant, as we have seen, that bears today can talk to us, ask for honey or tell us stories. They may also sing lullabies to put us to sleep or even launch into renderings of the 'Teddy Bears' Picnic'.

What Peter Bull called his 'most unfavourite refinement' in this area was a bear with a transistor tape concealed in its head. The owner could press one button and speak to the bear, then press another button, upon which the eyes would light up and the bear speak the very same words back in a voice transformed into a gravelly growl. Of such mutations Mr Bull had this to say:

Their very modernity turns them into some slightly spookey animal who is neither one thing nor the other and of whom one can never be sure. One can't imagine them listening or just Being Quiet. Friendship seems to be out of the question because in some way they attract too much attention to themselves.

Peter Bull feared that the manufacturers would never cease trying to demonstrate how they were managing to keep up with the times, and each new season in the toy trade will doubtless see many fresh wonders unveiled. True arctophiles, one suspects, will always tend to remain sceptical of whether the specifically new can ever add anything of much significance to the basic legend.

LEFT: *The profile of this teddy bear highlights his stitched nose and worn muzzle.*

THE GENERAL APPROACH

WHO GOES out and buys a bear? Parents do, of course. It is a most important matter, buying a bear by proxy for any infant, of whose life it will be a part for a long time to come. The basic fact of buying a bear shows an instinctive wish for the child to enjoy, as it grows, a fundamental sense of safety and security in its home background. The sort of teddy bear chosen in the meantime reveals as much about the psychology of the purchaser as does the choice of a certain breed or personality of dog. There never was such a wide range of bears available in stores and toy shops as there is today. All kinds of cultural and economic influences may come into play in deciding which to choose.

Such bears are, of course, bound for the hurly-burly of domestic life and are likely to find themselves in the thick of it. How many of them will survive to make vintage bears themselves in 50 years' time is anybody's guess. Whatever becomes of them, they will have served their cause well and will depart the scene honourably if they have simply been well-loved.

The motives of adults who buy bears for themselves may be different from or similar to those involved in buying bears for children. Many a hug of bears has its origin in one particular brand-new or well-worn bear that suddenly touched the heart-strings and prompted an impulse to buy. It may well be that there are people around today who would buy a bear purely for what they hope will be its rising value as an investment, but somehow, one feels, any self-respecting bear would find a subtle way of melting such stoney-hearted calculation. The reason discovered by Peter Bull to be more common than could possibly be imagined for buying a bear was to compensate for having suffered the loss of a bear in earlier years. This could be through accident, theft or the actions of well-meaning but over-anxious parents who decide that the time has arrived for Bears To Be Grown Out Of.

The development that has drawn the arctophile into the ranks of serious collectors is, however, a relatively recent one. A hobby that was

RIGHT: *Three bears representing the different sizes to be found.*

probably regarded before as a harmless eccentricity has earned respect and even taken on more than a touch of glamour through the high prices now being fetched for certain vintage bears in the sale rooms. As a consequence, the arctophile needs to become less of a happy-go-lucky amateur and more of a precisely informed specialist. There is a certain mystique attached to the world of the dealers, but well-informed amateur enthusiasts can always hold their own provided they do their homework.

The history of bears meanwhile continues to unfold and continues to have its obscure corners.

The first task facing the would-be collector is to get to know the signs, qualities and other pointers which indicate that a bear is of a certain make or period, as well as to know what makes some types rarer and hence more sought after than others. After that the would-be-collector must decide whether to remain a generalist, gathering together bears of all periods on a basis of personal response; or whether to specialize in, say, miniature bears or musical-box bears or even perhaps those ursine aristocrats, the teddies manufactured 50 or more years ago by the firm of Steiff. In fact the opportunities for

RIGHT: *A German bear, c 1910, with long arms, tapered ankles and flat feet.*

ABOVE: *The profile of the 1910 German bear shown above.*

specialization, too, have never been wider than they are today. Any individual collector will be governed by his or her own temperament, but a nice mix is probably the most attractive option.

· · · · · · GETTING TO KNOW · · · · ·
YOUR BEARS
· ·

From all that has been said it follows that self-education should be seriously considered, but, given the nature of the subject, the process should be kept enjoyable. Your simple objective is to be able to judge what it is you are looking at. In a thoroughly relaxed way, you can start to do this through illustrated books on teddies (of which you are soon bound to start building up a small library). The present interest in recent social history has led to an increase in the number of museums of toys and childhood. There are now several museums devoted entirely to teddy bears. It will be well worth the trouble to

visit as many of these establishments as you possibly can. The museums often publish excellent information packs or catalogues of their own collections. They also have archives, and researchers interested in teddy bear scholarship can apply to see them.

You should keep an eye on your local auction houses' announcements for any sales of dolls and bears. Collections of auctioneers' catalogues can build up into useful sources of information, especially if you have attended the auction yourself and been able to note down a record of prices fetched in the margin. Major auction rooms such as Sotheby's and Christies in London, of course, mainly take on the most rare and extravagant bears at the top end of the market. If you are actually buying, then there are advantages in visiting provincial sale rooms as prices will be lower there and the range of bears coming under the hammer will be wider and less predictable. Catalogue descriptions, however, may not be so reliable since local firms will not, like the metropolitan auction houses, have their own teddy bear expert. Keep it in mind that, generally speaking, the onus of responsibility is on bidders at auctions to satisfy themselves that the object being sold is genuinely what the auctioneer claims it to be.

The market in bears, as we have said, has been deliberately created, whether or not we like to think of it in this way. The market price of any period bear is defined in the auction rooms, and these prices always tend to rise. If you manage to buy the bear your heart most desires at an auction, remember that you will be obtaining it nott at a 'bargain' price but at the price that is current for that level of the market. You may even be paying rather more than that if you get carried away in the bidding, as is quite likely when it comes to bears. Remember, too, that many auction houses today impose the so-called buyer's premium of ten per cent on top of whatever a bid happens to reach. Strictly speaking you should always go into an auction with a clear idea of what you ought to be paying, or can afford to pay, for a certain bear, and be disciplined enough to drop out of the bidding if it rises beyond your limit. This is how the dealers function, but then their living depends on judging what they can charge in shops or other outlets to show a margin of profit.

Some people are daunted by the idea of attending an auction if they have never been to one before. If you feel nervous about the prospect, then go along to one or two appropriate auctions, just to sit in on them and quietly observe how they work. You will soon pick up the gist of the process. It is a myth that blinking an eye at the wrong moment may land you with an item you never wanted. You will notice that all the dealers and buyers have their own bidding manner. If you are seriously intending to bid, then study the auctioneers' conditions of sale carefully. These will be printed in the catalogue. A banker's reference may be required for bids over a certain amount. It is also a good idea to introduce yourself to the auctioneer before the bidding starts, especially if he does not know you.

These days prices tend to go out of date very quickly. It is therefore up to you to keep abreast of the main trends. In Britain, the *Lyle Official Antiques Review*, an annual publication, usually shows a selection of teddy bears, with prices, auctioned in the previous year, and the

ABOVE: *A typical English bear of the 1930s, sporting a green silk scarf.*

LEFT: *The same bear in profile, with the scarf removed to show the neck joint.*

34

ABOVE RIGHT: *A profile shot of the 'Little Charmer'*

BELOW RIGHT *This Chad Valley bear of the 1930s shows both the Aerolite button in the right ear and the rounding and softening of the muzzle and general body outline in this period.*

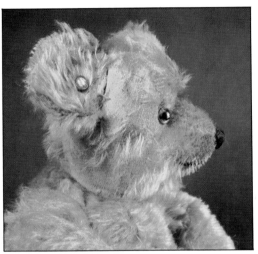

same firm's companion volume in its *Antiques and Their Values Series: Dolls and Toys*, is also reissued regularly in an updated edition. Apart from this, you can ask for price lists from specialist sales and watch the press, who will always make much of any outrageous price achieved. From time to time, toy and bear fairs are arranged and provide opportunities to buy or sell, look and chat and generally keep up to date. The specialist vintage toy and teddy shops also give clear indications of price trends by what they feel able to charge to collectors. Remember, however, that their prices may well reflect some costs for repair or restoration.

The advantages of buying at bear or toy fairs or in specialist shops are, of course, the range of types of bear from many periods that you will find to choose from as well as the chance of a surprise discovery that may irresistibly fill a

gap in your collection or set you going in an entirely fresh direction. As far as price trends are concerned, the Steiff bears remain the star attractions of the sale rooms, but it is noticeable that British bears from 50 or so years ago, like those made by Farnell, Chad Valley or Merrythought, have begun to rise in the price league, indicating a growing interest among collectors.

IDENTIFICATION

From the earliest days of the teddy bear craze there was a proliferation of manufacturers, many of whom came and went and whose names fell into oblivion. There are also manufacturers who are known from advertisements or other commercial ephemera or records but examples of whose bears have never been positively identified. Originally the great majority of teddies must have come with a tag, a trade label or token, such as the Steiff ear-button, but it is quite a rare event for these to survive in company with the bear. Many must have been discarded when the bear was first bought, and it would have been most unlikely for the original owner to have sewn an accidentally attached label back on again.

The linked questions of authentication and identification are therefore not always easy ones. Would-be collectors must keep many aspects in mind as they develop an eye for summing up a bear. They certainly need to be familiar with the evolution of the typical teddy bear profile over the course of its history. They also need to absorb as much knowledge as possible of the leading teddy bear manufacturers and what the main individual characteristics of their products have been at various times. If they are collecting recent as distinct from vintage bears, then they should also be *au fait* with technical developments in materials and manufacturing techniques. The very first all-washable 'safe eye' bear was introduced in the 1950s, for instance, by Wendy Boston Playsafe Toys. With recent bears, of course, the documentation becomes altogether more reliable and accessible.

The whole area of teddy scholarship has its vagueness and contradictions, and there is scope for anyone to research the original records and emerge with some hard facts. Judging a bear's age or identifying its make depends mainly on experience and common sense. The use of

traditional materials in fact changes relatively seldom. From the 1920s onwards, for instance, kapok often replaced wood wool as stuffing in British bears. Synthetic fur materials or plastic eyes will usually indicate a post-Second World War bear, but natural materials are still often used to make the best quality bears.

In Britain, the system of numbering designs registered with the Patent Office can be a useful researcher's tool for tracing makers and dates, though this is mostly relevant to bear-associated objects like china or novelty items such as pyjama cases.

· · · · · SOME LEADING MAKERS · · · · · OF BEARS

The Profile of the 'classic bear' from which all later developments spring has been described in Chapter Two. The following are among the most important firms to have contributed to that history (in order of their founding):

J. K. FARNELL Farnell's were one of the most senior family firms to specialize in the manufacture of stuffed toys, having been in business since 1840. They operated as a sort of family cottage industry in Acton, west London, until their Alpha Works factory was built adjacent to the family house at the end of the First World War. It is said to have been a Farnell 'Alpha' bear that Dorothy Milne bought for her little son Christopher at Harrods. Farnell's had started out by making toy animals from rabbit skins, but they also seem to have been pioneers in the use of Yorkshire plush fabric for stuffed animals. There are indications (never finally proven) of a link between Farnell's and Steiff when it came to originating the plush bear. Certainly the Farnell bears were very close to the Steiff pattern. The business was closed down in 1934 after a terrible fire had swept through the Farnell house and put the factory out of operation, but one of their former directors, J. C. Janisch, had by that stage already founded the Shropshire firm of Merrythought (see below).

STEIFF COMPANY The year 1880 is the official foundation date for Steiff, though Margarete Steiff had been carrying on her small business from home for several years previously. The importance of being familiar with Steiff bears,

the way their body shapes have evolved since 1903 and the various shades and types of plush that have been used in making them, can hardly be over-emphasized. They are the standard against which all other bears may ultimately be judged, being both highly individual and influential. The expert will always be able to identify a Steiff original, whether or not it has its ear-button. Steiff buttons and labels, where they do survive on a bear, convey a good deal of coded information on date, type and materials used. The Steiff museum at Giengen is a place of wonder and pilgrimage for all arctophiles.

CHAD VALLEY Although this company had its origins with a printing works in the 1820s, the key date in its history is 1897, the year in which it moved into new premises in the valley of the river Chad on the south-west outskirts of Birmingham. It was not until the First World War, however, that it began to manufacture dolls and soft toys, taking advantage of the gap in the market created by the blocking of German imports. The trade name of 'Chad Valley' was adopted in 1919, and their own line in teddy bears began to be manufactured from about 1920 onwards in a range of sizes and qualities. The earliest Chad Valley bears bore a metal trade button, usually though not invariably clipped to the ear, that carried the legend 'Chad Valley British Hygienic Toys'. They also had a label stitched underneath one foot. The labels, which have gone through a number of variations in wording over the years, are the main indicators to authenticate a Chad Valley bear. Chad Valley were the makers of the commercial version of Harry Corbett's Sooty.

IDEAL TOY COMPANY This is the senior firm of all American manufacturers of teddy bears, being the descendant of the Ideal Novelty and Toy Company, set up after 1903 to capitalize on the instant success of Maurice Mitchtom's original 'Teddy's bear'. There are unfortunately some quite considerable problems in identifying Ideal bears, owing to the fact that there never seems to have been a company policy to tag or label their teddies. Ideal bears tend to look, in fact, very like Steiff bears, though the experienced assessor will be aware of small differences of detail. For example, the ears tend to be large and set fairly low on the head, and the feet to be slightly pointed.

FACING PAGE: *These two Merrythought bears both date from the 1930s, but are very different in type, as their profiles (RIGHT AND FAR RIGHT) also demonstrate. The one sitting down has a button on his left shoulder which may be clearly seen in his profile portrait.*

DEAN'S Dean's Rag Book Company Ltd, founded in the south London borough of Merton in 1903, is today Britain's oldest surviving manufacturer of teddy bears. Among its other toys and products, the company has continued to produce a fine line of teddies based on vintage designs.

HERMANN After Steiff, Hermann is the best-known manufacturer of teddies, having been founded in 1907 specifically to make bears. An early Hermann bear is a rare animal and hard to distinguish from a Steiff. Later on another branch of the company included all kinds of other sorts of doll among its products. The present-day Hermann range includes traditional 'nostalgic' bears, 'No-No' bears (which were like the 'Yes-No' bears but only turned their heads from side to side and a musical box bear which plays 'The Teddy Bears Picnic'.

SCHREYER & CO. This Nuremberg company, formed in 1912, was responsible for the famous Schuco miniature bears, the 'Yes/No' bear and clockwork bears of various abilities. Its history has been outlined in Chapter Three, as has that of the other best-known maker of mechanical bears, Gebrüder Bing, which marketed its products, also from Nuremberg, from the early 1900s.

MERRYTHOUGHT The word 'merrythought' is an antique English term for a wishbone, and that is the trade name and sign of this company, founded in 1930 in the Shropshire town of Ironbridge. Very early Merrythought bears

carry a Steiff-like trade button in the ear, but this soon gave way to a label sewn on to one foot. Merrythought came into being to exploit the use of traditional Yorkshire plush material and was sponsored by a firm of mohair spinners who realized that the new synthetic fibres, such as rayon, represented a threat to their market. Ever since it was founded, Merrythought has enjoyed a reputation for making traditional bears of high quality. A Merrythought exhibition, associated with the Ironbridge Museum, is a source of pleasure to visitors.

INSTANT COLLECTABLES

No leading manufacturer of soft toys is today without its line in teddy bears. There are many bears of fine quality available, both as mass-market products and from workshops specializing in individually hand-crafted toys. From the infant's viewpoint, industrial standards of safety mean that the bear has never been a safer companion. From the collector's viewpoint, there never were so many choices competing for attention.

The essential romanticism of collectors has always led them to take a delight in the way a bear's rought-and-tumble nursery history moulds its battered but unbowed character. It may therefore seem a strange irony that a child's toy can become altogether too valuable an item to be allowed to fall into the hands of children. This, however, is what has happened in the area of designer craft bears or replica bears in limited editions which are made with a specific

RIGHT: *This example of a reproduction bear by Judy Sparrow is traditional even to the hump on the back, as the profile (BELOW) shows.*

eye to the collector's market. The traditional collector is likely to view these creations, however handsome they may be, as rather cold fish, and naturally enough, such bears tend to be quite expensive to buy in the first place. Afterwards they need to be maintained in mint condition if they are to remain valuable or possibly rise in value and prove to have been a good investment for their owners.

Steiff were quick to take up the idea of a reproduction vintage bear and in 1980 issued their centenary golden plush bear in a world-wide edition of 11,000 to commemorate their first hundred years of existence as a company. The teddy bear 80th anniversary year of 1983 saw several special issues, one of these being a handsome Steiff bear in silver grey mohair.

Merrythought weighed in with a 'Diamond Jubilee' bear that was a precise replica of the first golden bear they made in 1930. Fitted with a growler, it was limited to 1,000 bears and was exclusive to Harrods.

This section of the collectors' market is certainly an ever-expanding one at the moment, encouraged by the theory that, as soon as an edition of a particular bear has sold out, then the individual bears can be expected to start appreciating in value. Bears are at least a good deal more fun and better for the soul than many other areas of high finance.

Steiff continue to keep their replicas coming on to the market, and of course they have an unrivalled bank of historical and famous bears on which to draw. One of the more interesting of their recent issues is Alfonzo, limited to an edition of 5,000 and exclusive to the shop 'Teddy Bears' of Witney in Oxfordshire, who are the owners of the original. This is an example of a replica which reproduces the 'worn look'. Alfonzo was in May 1989 the proud holder of the world record price for a teddy bear, having been sold at Christie's for £12,100 ($22,000). In fact his record was startlingly eclipsed only four months later by the £55,000 ($100,000) Steiff bear sold at Sotheby's.

In the case of Alfonzo, a small perky bear only 13 inches (32 cm) high and dressed in silk Cossack-style tunic and trousers, his red mohair plush made him a great rarity, but on top of that he benefitted from a romantic provenance. He had belonged to the Princess Xenia Georgievna, a second cousin of the last Tsar of Russia who happened to be staying with the British Royal Family when the Russian Revolution broke out in 1917. Thus Alfonzo escaped the consequences of that historic upheaval and settled down to a life of exile in Britain.

We cannot all become the owners of original vintage Steiffs, and replicas are certainly one way of taking a direct delight in the value and beauty of much of the original workmanship. The bear on the ottoman is more immediate and personal to us than the bear in the museum. Not all limited edition bears are replicas, however. The House of Nisbet, for instance, who worked with the late Peter Bull on various ursine projects, have put out a number of original issues, usually of 5,000 each. They include one of a small Peter Bull bear called 'Bully Minor' and another of Aloysius alias Delicatessen. In the field of replication, Nisbet have also issued a Schuco 'Yes/No' bear. The bears designed by Sue Quinn for her company Dormouse Designs in Scotland may also be cited among limited edition originals of special character, only a few hundred of each design having been manufactured.

Even the experts are hard put to it to explain how the world's currently most expensive bear, a Steiff dating from the 1920s, can have made the sensational price of £55,000 ($100,000) at a Sotheby auction in September 1989. The result seems to have come about through two keen bidders showing an equal determination. Given the present climate of collectors' fever, we therefore constantly need to remind ourselves that what we are dealing with is only a child's toy, not an old master. The collector should certainly keep a serious eye open for those bears that are simply and humbly available in the shops. Nowadays Britain, the United States and Europe all have a thriving craft industry in bears of character. You will soon come to know the names of the firms, workshops or designers whose bears you happen to find personally attractive.

In buying modern bears, as in buying any bear, the question of quality is paramount, both in terms of design and of manufacture. The same rules apply here as in any other area of collecting. You should keep within the limits of what you can afford and the motive of individual appeal should be placed above other considerations. If you buy well then you buy for lasting pleasure, and in 50 or so years' time when your collection of 'vintage' bears is auctioned at Sotheby's, your grandchildren may well thank you for it. Remember, though, to keep safely all documentation relating to a purchase as well as associated tags or labels or other publicity material, for it always adds greatly to the interest and importance of any item to have its provenance fully preserved.

BELOW: *A Dean's Rag Book label* in situ *on the foot of a polar bear teddy.*

ASSESSING THE DAMAGE

THE WORDS 'much loved' in an auctioneer's catalogue, when they are used to describe a teddy bear, have come to be a euphemism for 'worn and torn'. Again we need to remind ourselves that the purchaser is buying a child's toy, not a work of art. A certain amount of wear and tear is inevitable in an old bear, though it sometimes happens that you do come across one which has never been played with, perhaps because the child died before it was old enough to enjoy it. Summing up the condition of a bear you are thinking of buying need take only a little practice.

If a bit of restoration work has already been carried out, then this will usually be obvious. When you are buying at auction, however, there is something to be said for buying a bear in an unrestored state so that you can judge, from your own observation, exactly what needs to be

done. A tear in the fabric can be patched, and lost stuffing can be made good. A missing ear or eye can be restored, wool stitching can be put back where it belongs and worn-through pads can be re-covered. None of these tasks is too daunting for the amateur.

It is possible for a bear to be over-restored, either if unsympathetic or unsuitable materials have been used, or if the repair work obscures the original expression or tampers with the proportions of the body or limbs. An attempt to restore an old bear's original colour (which can usually be seen by checking under the arms) would likewise come under the heading of over-restoration. The objective of restoration should never be to cover up or 'correct' those details which give us clues to a bear's life history. If your bear has a head that leans a little to one side or a rather squashed muzzle or a patch of fur worn down with hugging, then that is part of its charm and no true arctophile would wish to correct it. A bear that has been over-restored

ABOVE: *A well-preserved Schuco clockwork tumbling bear from the 1920s.*

LEFT: *A restored bear with unusually luxuriant fur.*

should always be avoided if you find it offered for sale.

Of course, the less that is wrong with a bear, then the more expensive it is going to be to buy. Vintage bears with growlers still in working condition, for instance, are naturally scarcer than those whose growlers have ceased to work. There is always a certain ratio between value and condition in the context of a bear's make or period. So far as the purchaser is concerned the basic adage cannot be over-emphasized: go for what appeals to you, pay no more than you can afford and avoid keeping the notion of 'investment' too much in mind.

· · · · · · · · BEAR REPAIR · · · · · · ·
· ·

In what circumstances can you undertake your own repair work, and when should you seek the help of experts? If you have been shockingly

extravagant and bought yourself an ursine aristocrat costing a small fortune then it goes without saying that you ought to seek expert advice before tampering with it in any way. With less expensive but nevertheless highly desirable bears, on the other hand, there is a good deal of domestic first aid that is practicable for the amateur to consider.

In the life of a bear, patches are as honourable as scars on a soldier. The first important principle, though, is to conserve old materials wherever you can and to match new materials as closely as possible with the old in terms of colouring and texture. If a tear in the fabric needs repairing, then a patch can be neatly stitched over it. If stuffing needs to be replaced, then the same sort of padding should be used, whether it be wood wool, kapok or something else. (Wood wool, incidentally, always seems to make for the sturdiest bears.) Pads often show signs of wear, especially if they are made from

44

felt. Using a thin matching felt, these should be replaced over the top of the original. If the felt needs to be moulded to fit, then it can first be steamed gently over a kettle.

It quite often happens that one ear has been lost somewhere along the way. In that case, you can carefully unpick the surviving ear to produce two identical and more or less semi-circular halves. These, relined with matching or toning felt, can then form the outer parts for a pair of ears that may be sewn back into position on the head. Treating all conserved and new materials against moths, especially if they are wool or mohair, is a sensible precaution.

Restoring black wool stitching for nose, mouth and claws is one of the simplest tasks. Eyes are rather more complicated, but matching sets of glass eyes are easy to come by and not difficult to insert or 'spike'. For an older bear, where boot-button eyes may be in character and authentic, you will need to go to some extra trouble to track them down in shops specializing in 'bygones'. Once you have found a supply, they are simple to sew into position.

A particularly serious problem can occur with jointed bears when the cardboard discs that rotate, and so allow a limb to move, rub against and wear through the fabric, so that the limb gets detached. You should inspect any prospective bear carefully to check that this is not happening or about to happen, for here is a problem that even the experts find a challenge.

BELOW: A bear repair kit includes spare eyes as well as discs for movable heads and limbs and a growler.

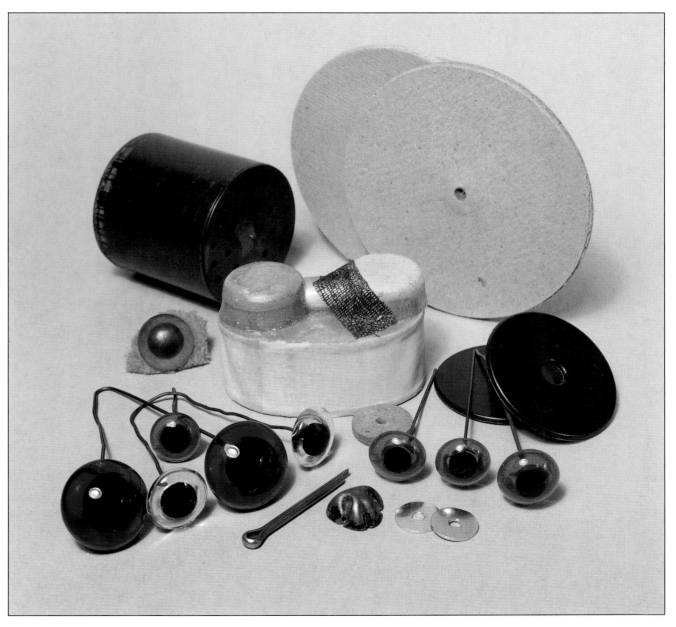

LEFT: *Skating bear, dressed for sport and ready for anything.*

RIGHT: *Can teddy bears grow to resemble their owners?*

If you do take on a bear suffering from this symptom, then you should be aware that it can involve a costly repair; and if a limb does come adrift, then do be careful not to lose it.

· · · · · · · · · BEAR CARE · · · · · · · · ·
· ·

Teddy bears make wonderful homes for all sorts of pests. Mice, for example, will see a vintage bear, stuffed with excelsior wood wool, as a first-class dwelling. You will need to guard against the disaster which mice could represent, especially if you have to store a bear away for a while for any reason. Bears may also act as host to mites, fleas, silver fish and the dreaded eggs and larvae of the clothes moth. For a newly acquired bear, or even a bear you have had for some time but never treated, it is a good idea to follow Pam Hebbs's advice and place him, sealed in a plastic

bag, for at least two days in a freezer. When you take him out, any condensation can be dried off with a hair dryer on a low setting and his fur carefully brushed. A general moth-proofing is then advisable to ward off further attacks, but any enemies previously present will have been brought to account.

Bears are great dust traps, so they should be gently brushed over every now and then. Keep a special brush to brush out the fur of your bears, for human hair oils do not make good contacts for plush or mohair fibres. The brush should have firm but not harsh or scratchy bristles. It is possible, Pam Hebbs also advises, to shampoo a bear, provided that great care is exercised. The mildest possible fabric shampoo should be sparingly used, slightly diluted and teased lightly into the fur with a nail brush, using circular motions. After towelling the bear with a soft towel, repeat the process with tepid water that contains a recom-

LEFT: *The ultimate accolade for a teddy bear is a child's affection.*

mended proportion of fabric conditioner. Towel the bear once more and then dry with a hair dryer set to give a low heat, brushing delicately as the process continues. Finally the bear can be kept in an airing cupboard for a couple of days before being given a last brisk brushing over.

Damp and light are enemies that the arctophile has in common with the art collector as they may both be as harmful to bears as they can be to pictures. Each hazard is to be avoided. The damage that damp can do is obvious, but light will fade the colour pigments of a fabric (it will probably already have done so on a vintage bear) and direct sunlight may hasten the decay process in natural fibres. Bears are best kept in a shaded position in a room that has a normal level of warmth and humidity.

You will also need to guard your bears against the attentions of other family members, parti-

cularly if there is a cat or a dog who may see them as comfortable cushions. And always put your favourite or valuable bears out of sight before friends with small children visit you. The children will expect to be allowed to play with the bears as soon as they see them, and the parents will expect you to let them do so – quite probably with horrible results. If you often have visits from young families, it may be a good plan to maintain a second-division hug of knockabout bears simply for entertainment purposes.

The last protection to consider is insurance. In every area of collecting, values creep up, and you should double-check with your insurance agent or broker on whether your bear collection needs to be specially listed under your household cover. This seems a wise precaution in times when the value of even one bear can reach considerable heights.